CCSS **Genre** Biography

Essential Question
What do heroes do?

Rudy Garcia-Tolson

by Ann Weil

Chapter 1

A Hero Who Has No Legs

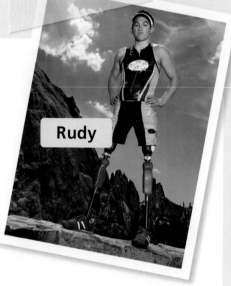

Rudy

Rudy Garcia-Tolson was not born a hero. But by age 8, Rudy was a hero to many people. He faced challenges when he was born. But this did not stop him from becoming a strong athlete.

Rudy was born with **birth defects**. He had problems with his mouth and his hands. But the most serious problems were with his legs. Everyday tasks were hard for Rudy.

Jason Dewey Photography

Rudy wanted to be able to walk and play. Doctors tried to fix some of the problems with his legs. But they could not fix everything. Rudy had many **operations,** but his legs still had problems. Doctors told Rudy they could give him new legs. First they would need to remove his old legs. Rudy and his family decided he would have the operation.

Doctors help people who are feeling sick or are in pain.

doctor

patient

When Rudy was five years old, doctors removed his legs. Then the doctors gave him artificial legs. They were made of plastic and metal. They were very strong. Now Rudy could run and walk.

artificial leg

Artificial arms and legs let people without legs or hands walk and hold things.

STOP AND CHECK

What have you learned about Rudy so far?

Chapter 2

New Legs, New Start

helmet

Rudy's new legs helped him to try many sports.

Rudy's new legs gave him courage. He tried new sports. He learned to swim. He could even ride a bike! Then Rudy began to discover a new interest. He wanted to become a great athlete. He wanted to show people that he could do many of the same things they could. This made Rudy a hero.

Terry Martin/Rudy Garcia-Tolson

goggles

Rudy can swim faster than many swimmers with two legs.

Rudy loved to swim. He felt free in the water. Rudy did not need his new legs for swimming. Rudy did not <u>kick</u> underwater. He swam using his strong arms and upper body. He could swim quickly. He became a great swimmer.

Rudy entered swimming races. He won first place in many races.

Language Detective	<u>Kick</u> is an action verb. Find another action verb on this page.

Rudy also competed in **triathlons**. These are races where people swim, bike, and run. First Rudy took off his legs to swim. Then he put on a special pair of legs to bike. After getting off the bike, Rudy put on new legs for running.

When Rudy was 10 years old, he finished a triathlon on his own. He was the youngest person without legs to do this.

Rudy wears special legs for each sport.

Rudy won a gold medal at the Paralympic Games in 2004.

Rudy set records in swimming. He won his first gold medal when he was only 16 years old. At age 18, he won a second gold medal at the Paralympic competition in Durban, South Africa. Rudy continues to set swimming records today.

STOP AND CHECK

What did Rudy do when he was 10 years old?

chapter 3 — An Athlete's Life

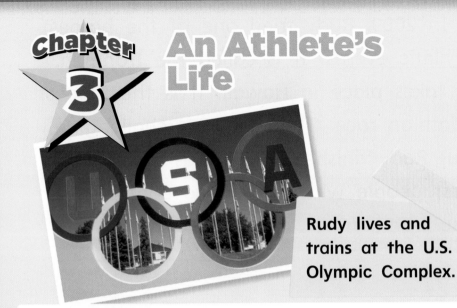

Rudy lives and trains at the U.S. Olympic Complex.

Rudy lives at a training center. He is able to practice and exercise there. He also meets with his doctors. The doctors study ways that they can improve Rudy's legs. With <u>their</u> help, Rudy can perform even better.

Living at the training center lets Rudy spend time with other athletes. He also eats healthful food. Rudy takes care of himself so he can succeed.

Language Detective

<u>Their</u> is a possessive pronoun. Find another possessive pronoun on this page.

In 2009, Rudy tried one of the hardest athletic events. It is called the Ironman. It takes place in Hawaii. It is the longest triathlon race. The race was challenging, but Rudy finished it. He was one of the first people with no legs to compete in the Ironman.

ocean

After swimming and biking, Rudy ran 26.2 miles to finish the race.

STOP AND CHECK

How does Rudy take care of himself at the training center?

Rudy is a hero to many kids.

wheelchair

Heroes do things to help others. Some heroes rescue people from dangerous places. Firefighters do that. People agree that Rudy is a different kind of hero. He is a **role model**. He inspires others. Rudy shows people that they can <u>go for</u> their dreams.

In Other Words reach for. En español: *lograr.*

Ariel Skelley/CORBIS

Rudy Garcia-Tolson

The Life of a Hero

1988 Rudy was born on September 14 in California.

1998 At age 10, Rudy became the youngest athlete with two artificial legs to do a triathlon on his own.

1985 •••• 1990 •••• 1995 •••• 2000 ••••

1993 Doctors removed both of Rudy's legs.

2003 *Teen People* magazine called Rudy one of "20 Teens Who Will Change the World."

2004 Rudy won the gold medal at the Paralympic Games in Greece.

564

139

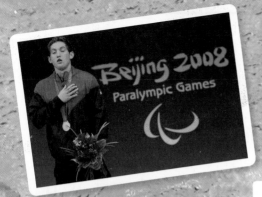

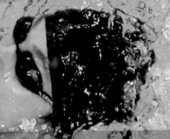

2012 His goal for 2012 was to be in his third Paralympic Games.

2005 •••• **2010** •••• **2015**

2007 Rudy moved to the Olympic Training Center.

2011 Rudy joined the U.S. team in the Pan-Pacific Para-Swimming Championships.

2008 Rudy won gold and bronze medals in swimming at the Paralympic Games in China.

Rudy always keeps a positive attitude and never gives up. He likes to share his story with people. He tells children and adults what he has learned.

Rudy's <u>motto</u> is, "A brave heart is a powerful weapon." This means that when you are not afraid, you can do anything.

In Other Words   phrase.
En español: *lema, frase.*

Rudy's success inspires others to do their best.

STOP AND CHECK

How does Rudy inspire others?

Respond to Reading

Summarize

Use important details to help you summarize *Rudy Garcia-Tolson*.

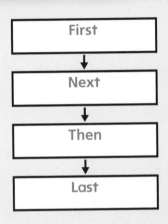

First

↓

Next

↓

Then

↓

Last

Text Evidence

1. How do you know *Rudy Garcia-Tolson* is a biography? Genre

2. What happened in Rudy's childhood that led him to become an athlete?

   Sequence

3. Figure out the synonym for the word *challenging* on page 10. Synonyms

4. Read the timeline. Write about what Rudy did in Greece in 2004.

   Write About Reading

Compare Texts
Read about another hero.

The Unsinkable Molly Brown

A legend is a story. It is part fact and part fiction. There are legends about heroes. One legend is about a hero named Molly Brown. The legend is based on a real person named Maggie Brown.

In 1912, Maggie Brown was on a ship called the *Titanic*. The *Titanic* sank at sea. Many people died. About 700 people, including Maggie, survived.

Maggie Brown lived from 1867 to 1932.

Taking Charge

Maggie was able to get into a lifeboat. Others were not so lucky. The lifeboat started to sail away. Maggie made the boat turn around. She wanted to look for more people in the water.

A big ship picked up the passengers in Maggie's lifeboat. Maggie was safe.

The *Titanic* sank in 1912.

The Legend

Maggie's actions made her a legend. Then someone wrote a musical about her. The writer thought *Molly* sounded better than *Maggie*. The result was a movie called "The Unsinkable Molly Brown."

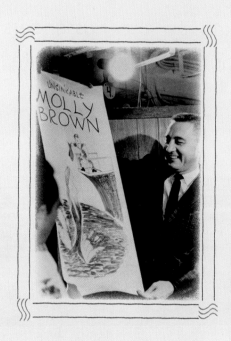

Movies about real people sometimes add made-up ideas and events to the story.

Make Connections

What are some things heroes do?

Essential Question

What makes Molly and Rudy brave?

Text to Text

Glossary

birth defects problems with a baby's body or mind when it is born *(page 2)*

operations surgeries performed by a doctor on a person's body to help the person get better *(page 3)*

role model a person whose good qualities are imitated by others *(page II)*

triathlons three-part races (usually swimming, biking, running) *(page 7)*

Index

Focus on
Social Studies

Purpose To identify a hero

What to Do

Step 1 Work with a partner. Make a poster with the title "My Hero."

Step 2 Write your hero's name. Then write three things your hero did to become your hero.

Step 3 Draw a picture of each action.

Step 4 Share your poster with the class.